# Oceans of the World

# Indian Ocean

Louise and Richard Spilsbury

**heinemann**
raintree

© 2015 Heinemann Raintree
an imprint of Capstone Global Library, LLC
Chicago, Illinois

To contact Capstone Global Library please
call 800-747-4992, or visit our web site
www.capstonepub.com

Edited by Penny West
Designed by Steve Mead
Original illustrations © Capstone Global Library Ltd 2015
Picture research by Tracy Cummins
Production by Victoria Fitzgerald
Originated by Capstone Global Library Ltd
Printed and bound in China by Leo Paper Group

18 17 16 15 14
10 9 8 7 6 5 4 3 2 1

Library of Congress Cataloging-in-Publication Data
Spilsbury, Louise.
  Indian Ocean / Louise Spilsbury and Richard Spilsbury.
    pages cm.—(Oceans of the world)
  Includes bibliographical references and index.
  ISBN 978-1-4846-0772-5 (hb)—ISBN 978-1-4846-0778-7 (pb)—ISBN 978-1-4846-0790-9 (ebook)  1. Oceanography—Indian Ocean—Juvenile literature. 2. Indian Ocean—Juvenile literature.  I. Spilsbury, Richard, 1963- II. Title.

  GC721.S75 2015
  910.9182'4—dc23                    2014010886

This book has been officially leveled by using the F&P Text Level Gradient™ Leveling System.

Acknowledgments
We would like to thank the following for permission to reproduce photographs: Alamy Images: Vito Arcomano, 10; Corbis: Construction Photography, 18, Lawson Wood, 8; iStockphoto: EirikE, 21; NASA: MODIS/Jeff Schmaltz, 14, Earth Observatory, Cover Middle; Science Source: Observer, 11; Shutterstock: Brian Kinney, 7, Daniel J. Rao, 15, Ekaterina Rainbow, 4, Em7, 19, erandamx, 22, Iakov Kalinin, 12, Cover Top, javarman, 13, Krzysztof Odziomek, 24, Liunian, 27, Nataliya Hora, 20, Oleksandr Kalinichenko, 26, Rich Carey, Cover Bottom, Rich Lindie, 16, Zmiter, Design Element; Thinkstock: Andrea Izzotti, 25, Zoonar/P.Malyshev, 17.

We would like to thank Michael Bright for his invaluable help
in the preparation of this book.

# Contents

Some words are shown in bold, **like this**. You can find out what they mean by looking in the glossary.

# About the Indian Ocean

The Indian Ocean is one of the world's five oceans. An ocean is a huge area of salty water. The Indian Ocean is the third-biggest ocean on Earth, after the Pacific and Atlantic.

The Indian Ocean covers about a fifth of the total area of ocean in the world.

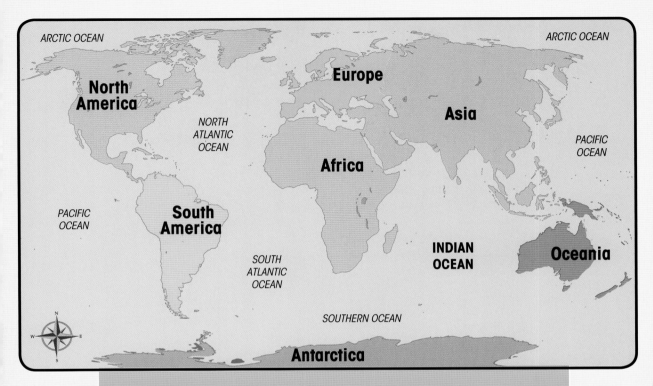

In the southwest, the Indian Ocean joins the Atlantic Ocean, and to the east it meets the Pacific Ocean.

The five oceans are joined and water flows between them. The oceans are mostly divided up by the seven **continents**. The Indian Ocean lies between the continents of Africa in the west, Oceania in the east, and Asia in the north.

The Indian Ocean is mostly wide open water, but it has other parts, too. The Bay of Bengal is the largest **bay** in the world. A bay is an area of ocean partly enclosed by land, with a wide opening where it joins the rest of the ocean.

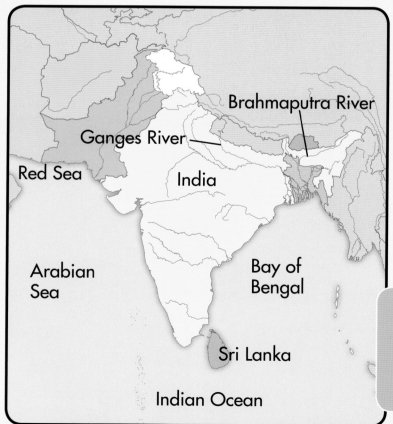

Large **rivers** such as the Ganges and Brahmaputra flow into the Bay of Bengal.

The Red Sea is a popular diving destination because its coastal waters are clear, warm, and rich in marine life.

**Seas** are smaller areas of ocean usually partly surrounded by land. The Arabian Sea is a large sea in the Indian Ocean. The Red Sea lies between the **continents** of Africa and Asia.

# Geography

The bottom of any ocean has dips and hills, just like on land. On the Indian Ocean floor, there are flat areas called plains and mountain chains called **ridges**. The Indian Ocean also has caves beneath its surface.

Divers swim and explore a rock cave in the Indian Ocean.

## Indian Ocean fact file

| | |
|---|---|
| Size: | About 5.5 times the size of the United States |
| Area: | 26,470,000 square miles (68,556,000 square kilometers) without its **seas** Coastline: 41,337 miles (66,526 kilometers) |
| Average depth: | 12,760 feet (3,890 meters) |
| Deepest point: | 24,442 feet (7,450 meters) in Java Trench near Java, Indonesia |

Seamounts are underwater mountains over 3,300 feet (1 kilometer) tall. They have flat tops and sloping sides. There are valleys called **trenches** on the ocean floor, too. The Java Trench is the biggest, at 2,000 miles (3,200 kilometers) long!

The Ganges and Brahmaputra **rivers** flow into the Indian Ocean. When river water enters an ocean, it slows and the **sediment** it was carrying sinks. This creates marshy, muddy areas of land called **deltas**. The Ganges–Brahmaputra Delta is the largest in the world.

Crops grow well in muddy, sediment-rich deltas, so there are millions of farmers on the Ganges–Brahmaputra Delta.

This is the Irrawaddy Delta in Myanmar. The sediment that the Irrawaddy River washes into the Indian Ocean forms piles on the ocean floor.

Some river sediment washes out into the ocean and sinks there. The pile of sediment from the Ganges–Brahmaputra stretches around 1,550 miles (2,500 kilometers) under the Indian Ocean and is up to 7 miles (11 kilometers) thick.

# Temperature

The Indian Ocean is the warmest ocean on Earth because a large part of it lies in the **Tropics**. This is the area that is closest to the **Equator**, an imaginary line around the center of Earth. The land and waters around the Equator are mainly warm throughout the year.

The surface water of the warmest parts of the Indian Ocean is as hot as a warm bath!

Around the coast of the Indian Ocean, people catch shrimp and fish such as skate.

**Plankton** are tiny living things that drift through oceans and provide food for fish and other animals. Fewer plankton live in warmer waters, so there are fewer fish in parts of the Indian Ocean than in other oceans.

# Weather

The Indian Ocean causes some extreme weather! Huge, whirling winds called **cyclones** happen when warm ocean water heats the air above it. When hot air rises quickly, it causes winds that spin very quickly. Cyclones can snap trees and damage buildings.

This photo, taken from a satellite up in space, shows the whirling winds of a fierce cyclone.

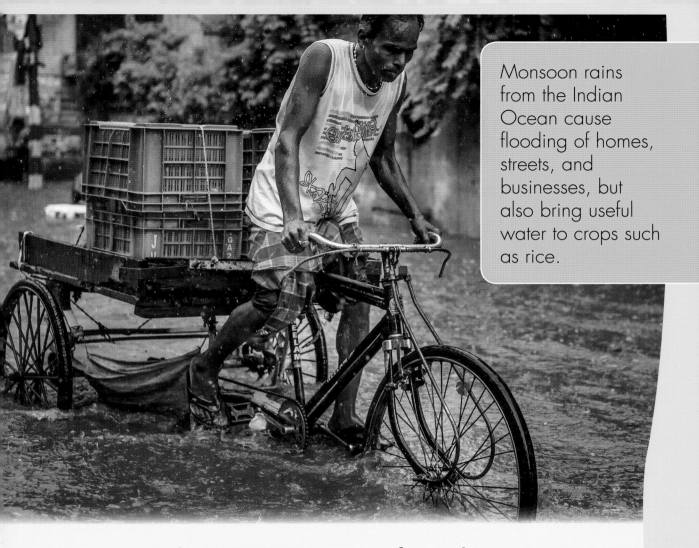

Monsoon rains from the Indian Ocean cause flooding of homes, streets, and businesses, but also bring useful water to crops such as rice.

In summer, the warm, moist air from the southwest Indian Ocean blows toward India, Sri Lanka, and Bangladesh. The moist air brings weeks of heavy rains, known as the **monsoon** season, to these areas.

# Islands

The Indian Ocean has many major islands. Madagascar became an island after it broke off from the **continent** of Africa 165 million years ago. Madagascar is the largest Indian Ocean island and the fourth largest in the world.

Madagascar has been cut off from Africa for so long that 80 percent of the animals on this island exist only here and nowhere else.

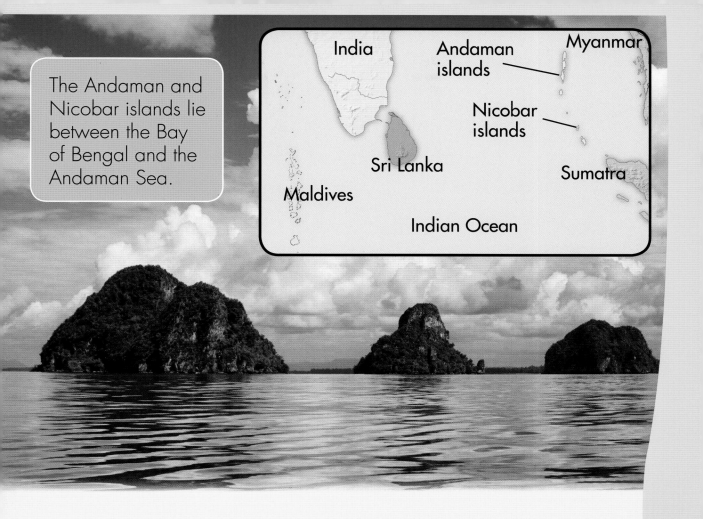

The Andaman and Nicobar islands lie between the Bay of Bengal and the Andaman Sea.

India

Andaman islands

Myanmar

Nicobar islands

Sri Lanka

Sumatra

Maldives

Indian Ocean

The Andaman and Nicobar islands are actually the tops of underwater mountains that rise up from the ocean floor and poke above the water. There are over 300 Andaman islands and 19 Nicobar islands.

# Resources

About 40 percent of the world's offshore oil is from rocks under the Indian Ocean and especially the Persian Gulf by Saudi Arabia. Each day ships called tankers transport enough oil to fill 1,000 Olympic swimming pools from this region across the Indian Ocean.

This giant tanker is transporting oil from the Persian Gulf to places where it is needed to power machines.

Sea salt is an ocean mineral people use to flavor foods. In this village in Thailand, people are making salt by letting pools of Indian Ocean seawater dry out.

People also collect and use **minerals** from around the Indian Ocean. They mine gravel and sand to use in concrete. They can also get certain metals, such as titanium, from some sand. Titanium can be used to make light, strong aircraft.

# Ports

A **port** is a place where ships load and unload. The port of Singapore is a busy port in the Indian Ocean. Most goods, including cars, clothes, and TVs, are transported in and out of Singapore in large metal boxes called containers.

Each year, Singapore port workers unload, store, and load 30 million containers!

Spices grown in Zanzibar and other places around the Indian Ocean are in demand around the world for flavoring foods.

Zanzibar is an Indian Ocean island that first grew wealthy by trading in valuable spices, such as cloves, from its port. Today, there are still spice markets, but there is also a modern container port.

# People

Hundreds of millions of people live and work along the Indian Ocean coastline. Some live in huge cities near busy **ports**, such as Mumbai in India. Others live in simple huts in small fishing or farming villages and make a living from the ocean.

These Sri Lankan fishermen stand on long poles to fish.

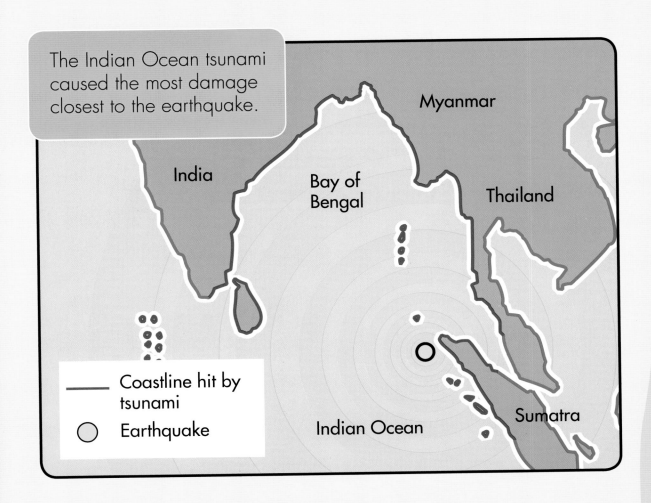

The Indian Ocean tsunami caused the most damage closest to the earthquake.

Myanmar

India

Bay of Bengal

Thailand

Indian Ocean

Sumatra

_____ Coastline hit by tsunami

◯ Earthquake

In 2004, an **earthquake** in the ocean floor caused huge waves in the Indian Ocean. These huge waves are called a **tsunami**. The tsunami flooded land and destroyed homes, boats, and roads all around the Indian Ocean coastline.

23

# Animals

The Indian Ocean is home to the biggest fish in the world. Whale sharks can reach 40 feet (12 meters) long! This giant animal opens its mouth wide to filter tiny **plankton** from the seawater to eat.

The whale shark is as big as a bus!

Some dugongs live in the shallow waters of the Red Sea and western Australia.

Dugongs and humpback whales also live in the Indian Ocean. Dugongs are often called sea cows because they graze on sea grass underwater. Some humpback whales live in this ocean year round and raise their calves in the warm waters.

# Famous Places

One of the most famous places in the Indian Ocean was made by people. The Suez Canal is a waterway built to connect the Red Sea and the Mediterranean Sea. It allows ships to travel between Europe and Asia without going around the entire **continent** of Africa.

Going through the Suez Canal shortens a boat trip from Mumbai to London by 5,600 miles (9,000 kilometers)!

The Maldives islands are famous for their white, sandy beaches and warm, turquoise water.

The Maldives islands in the Indian Ocean, south of India, are a famous tourist attraction. The Maldives are made up of 1,200 small coral islands. People live on only 200 of the islands, and 80 of the islands have tourist resorts.

# Fun Facts

- Around 80 percent of the Maldives are less than 3 feet (1 meter) above sea level. The sea level is rising by over 1 inch (about 3 centimeters) every 10 years. Scientists say much of the country could be underwater by the end of the 21st century.

- The Indian Ocean is the youngest in the world. It is around 80 million years old, which is less than half the age of the Pacific Ocean.

- Dugongs are close relatives of elephants. Scientists can tell this because the two animals have similar skeletons.

- Some waves in the Indian Ocean **tsunami** of 2004 were 98 feet (30 meters) high.

# Quiz

**1** What is the largest **bay** in the world?

**2** What is the wind that causes a rainy season in India and other parts of Asia in summer?

**3** Which is the largest island in the Indian Ocean?

**4** Which are the only two oceans bigger than the Indian Ocean?

**Answers**

**1** The Bay of Bengal is the largest bay in the world.

**2** The **monsoon** causes the rainy season.

**3** The largest island in the Indian Ocean is Madagascar.

**4** The Pacific and the Atlantic are bigger than the Indian Ocean.

# Glossary

**bay**  area of ocean partly enclosed by land with a wide opening to an ocean

**continent**  one of seven huge areas of land on Earth

**cyclone**  powerful storm with very fast winds that forms over warm water

**delta**  flat, muddy area created by a river where it meets an ocean

**earthquake**  sudden shaking of the ground

**Equator**  imaginary line around the middle of Earth

**mineral**  solid material found in the natural world that is not living, such as a metal

**monsoon**  winds from over the Indian Ocean that bring heavy rains to Asia

**plankton**  tiny living plants and animals floating in water

**port**  place at the edge of an ocean where ships stop

**ridge**  long, narrow crest linking the tops of a row of mountains

**river**  area of moving fresh water

**sea**  smaller area of an ocean usually found near the land and usually partly surrounded by land

**sediment**  mud, sand, and stones that can be carried by moving water

**trench**  long, narrow, and deep hole in the ground

**Tropics**  region of Earth's surface that is closest to the Equator

**tsunami**  long, high waves caused by an underwater earthquake

# Find Out More

## Books

Labrecque, Ellen. *Deep Oceans* (Earth's Last Frontiers). Chicago: Heinemann Library, 2014.

MacQuitty, Miranda. *Ocean* (DK Eyewitness). New York: Dorling Kindersley, 2013.

Markovics, Joyce L. *Tsunami* (It's a Disaster!). New York: Bearport, 2014.

Morgan, Sally. *Earth's Water Cycle* (Earth Cycles). Mankato, Minn.: Smart Apple Media, 2012.

## Web sites

Facthound offers a safe, fun way to find Internet sites related to this book. All of the sites on Facthound have been researched by our staff.

Here's all you do:
Visit www.facthound.com
Type in this code: 9781484607725

# Index